# ENTER THE DRAGON

## Photo Collection
## Volume One

"Enter the Dragon Photo Collection Volume One", by Rick Baker
Edited by Rick Baker. Foreword by Rick Baker
Photographs from the EH Archives

Special thanks to: K.Reeve, George Tan, Ting Wai Ho, Nic Cairns, Nick Singh,
Alan Donkin. And a special mention to Gary Burton who got me my first ticket
to see this movie, after five failed attempts for being under-age.
Special mention to my mum who was as big a kung fu movie fans as me.
Special thanks to Steve K for maintaining my love of Bruce Lee.
Special thanks to Sylvester (Sly) Raymond for being a good friend.

Special dedication to Chan Yuk. Thank you for the many images and moments in time you
left, of one of the greatest icons the world has even known – BRUCE LEE, 1940 – 1973

Every effort to trace the copyright holders of the illustrations and original layouts in this book.
In the event that any have been inadvertently overlooked, please contact the publishers
so that the situation can be rectified in future editions.

Please note: The photographs within these pages have been presented in their best quality format.
Some original negatives had slight damage and it was decided to leave them as seen for authenticity
(sometimes over exposed and slighty out of focus). Some contact sheets had light scratches due to
age. Printing on a matt paper can sometimes highlight these issues, but time and care has been taken
with the images used to give the reader the best quality presentation.

First published by Eastern Heroes 2020
www.easternheroes.com
FIRST EDITION

Printed by © Copyright 2020 Ingram Content Group, www.ingramspark.com. All Rights Reserved.
Design & Layout, Nic Cairns, 22:22 Creative Media

ISBN: 978-1-8380706-3-2

All rights reserved. No parts of this publication may be reproduced or transmitted in any
form or by any means, graphic, electronic or mechanical, including photocopying, recording,
taping or any information storage and retrieval system, without prior written permission of the
publisher.

# INTRODUCTION

**E**nter the Dragon **is, without doubt,** the most important and influential martial arts movie ever made. It is a film that inspired and influenced audiences around the globe, and introduced a new icon and superstar to the world – Bruce Lee.

"In the beginning the world had only flirted with martial art movies. It was not until Bruce Lee came along that the world fell in love with them."

# BIRTH OF A MOVIE

**D**espite his box office success in Hong Kong, American audiences had only been exposed to Bruce in a few TV appearances and his portrayal of Kato in *The Green Hornet*.

*Enter the Dragon* changed that. Yet, it was far from a comfortable experience. Bruce faced nerves, language barriers on set, and a script that was being constantly altered. Eventually, however, the film took shape, and the end result was a masterpiece ready to be unleashed onto a largely unsuspecting global audience.

On 19th August 1973, *Enter the Dragon* enjoyed its Hollywood premiere at Mann's Chinese Theatre. It was a co-production between Golden Harvest, Warner Brothers and Concord Productions Inc. As a movie with an international flavour, and the combined might of several companies behind it, *Enter the Dragon* was heavily advertised prior to its release. Despite the movie itself commanding a meagre budget of only US$850,000, the marketing budget was estimated to be in excess of US$1 million dollars. This was an unprecedented amount for a promotional campaign, and demonstrates how committed the backers were to make an international star out of Bruce Lee.

To advertise the movie, the studio offered free karate classes, and produced thousands of illustrated flip books, comic books, posters and photographs. *Enter the Dragon* memorabilia has now become very sought-after amongst collectors.

The PR departments also issued dozens of press releases for high-end publications, including *Esquire* and *The Wall Street Journal*. These prestigious outlets were largely uncharted waters for kung fu films. They also arranged public appearances for the stars, although due to Bruce's untimely death, the main attraction of the movie would not be present at these engagements.

The original screenplay title was *Blood and Steel*, and a young writer named Michael Allin was drafted in to write a script specifically tailored as a Bruce Lee vehicle. A cast of various mixed nationalities was envisaged, including Asian, white and black protagonists, in the belief that this would broaden the film's appeal to a much wider international audience.

Apparently, Lee clashed with Allin, with Lee demanding that the writer leave Hong Kong. Instead, Warner Bros producer Fred Weintraub moved him to another hotel in order to continue the script. When Bruce found out, he was furious, and was said to refuse to continue filming. Matters did obviously get smoothed out, but Bruce never forgave the producers.

Despite the behind the scenes chaos, the script was finished, and *Blood and Steel* became *Enter the Dragon*, a title that even if you haven't watched it, you've certainly heard of it, as well as the name of its star. *Enter The Dragon* has stood the test of time. Even as I write this, the film has just had two new releases, both on the Criterion Label and a special edition box set from HMV UK.

As I reflect back on this movie, it has had an extraordinary effect on many people. I for one can testify that, for me, the impact of the movie inspired me to pursue a career in the genre that has spanned four decades since that first screening back in the summer of 1974. Additionally, I would argue that this was one of the most photographed movies of all time. At an educated guess, there must be over 12,000 photos taken during that short movie shoot. Did those present know something we did not? That something truly special was unfolding before their eyes? With social media linking up Bruce Lee fans all over the world, we can marvel at the sheer volume of photographs circulating, and enjoy the constant stream of new information and stories that took place during filming. My books aim to provide you, the reader, with a selection of images to enjoy from this remarkable movie. Even with two volumes you can only show a fraction of the photographs that exist worldwide, but I will endeavour to showcase what are, in my view, the finest.

*Enter the Dragon* ended up being a worldwide success, taking over US$350 million at the box office over a series of releases, which is equivalent to approximately $1.2 billion in today's money. Measured against a cost-to-profit ratio, it is one of the most successful films of all time.

The success of the movie arguably boils down to one dominating factor: Bruce Lee. Without his star power, it would have paled into insignificance after its release. The photographs in this book reflect his magnetic charisma and screen presence, which drew so many people to the film.

In Volume Two, I will look in greater depth at the rest of the cast, and those famous faces in the movie that where undiscovered at the time of their appearances, but are now household names in Hong Kong cinema. I will also present another dynamic collection of photographs highlighting scenes in front of, and behind, the camera.

# BATTLE OF THE LEGENDS

These opening scenes captures Bruce Lee at his peak of stardom, an icon whose life was to be cut short by his untimely death. Opposing him is a young Sammo Hung, who was unknown in the West but who now has reached iconic status worldwide with his contribution to Hong Kong cinema as a choreographer, director and action star.

*Enter the Dragon* Photographic Collection – Vol. 1

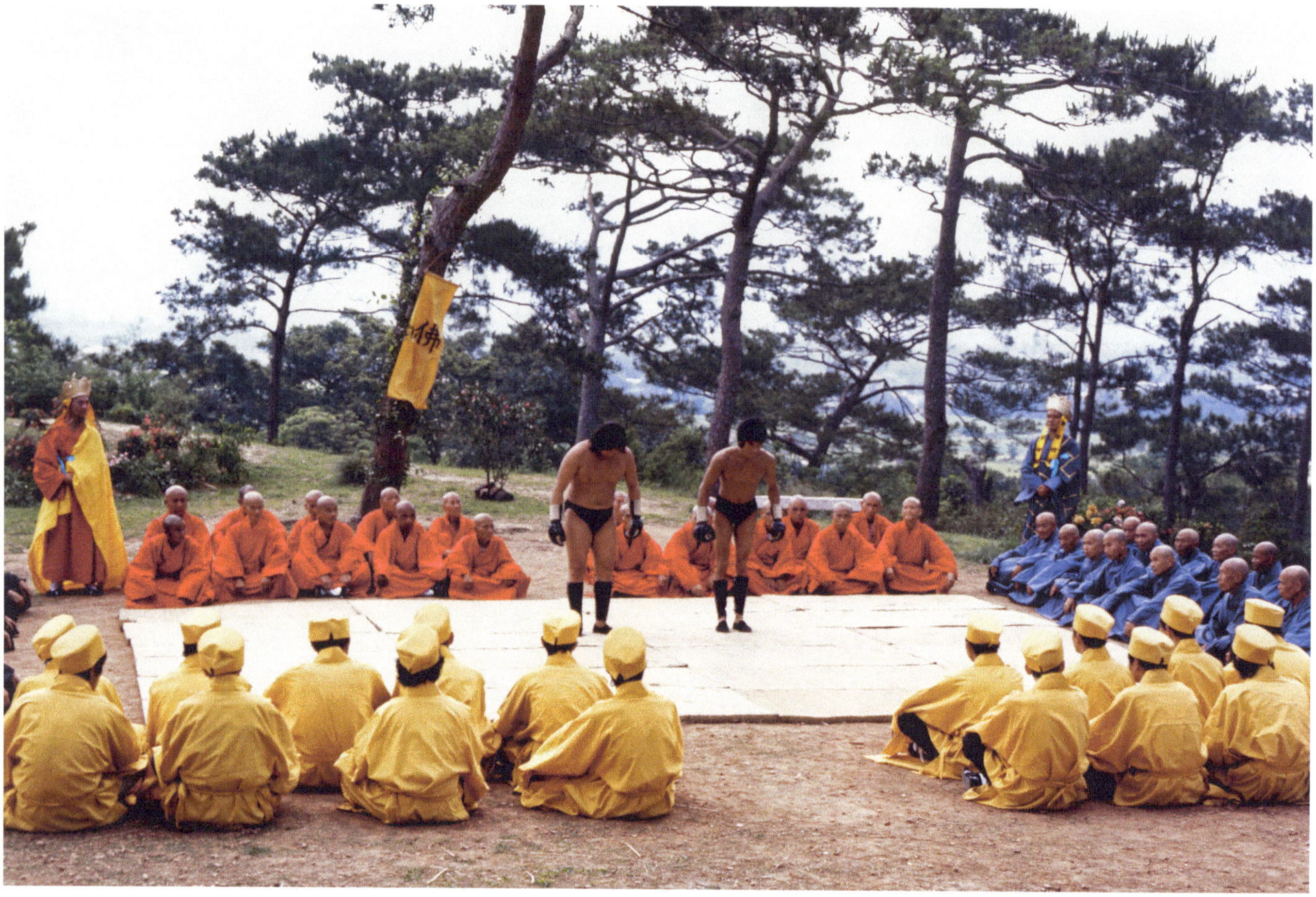
佛

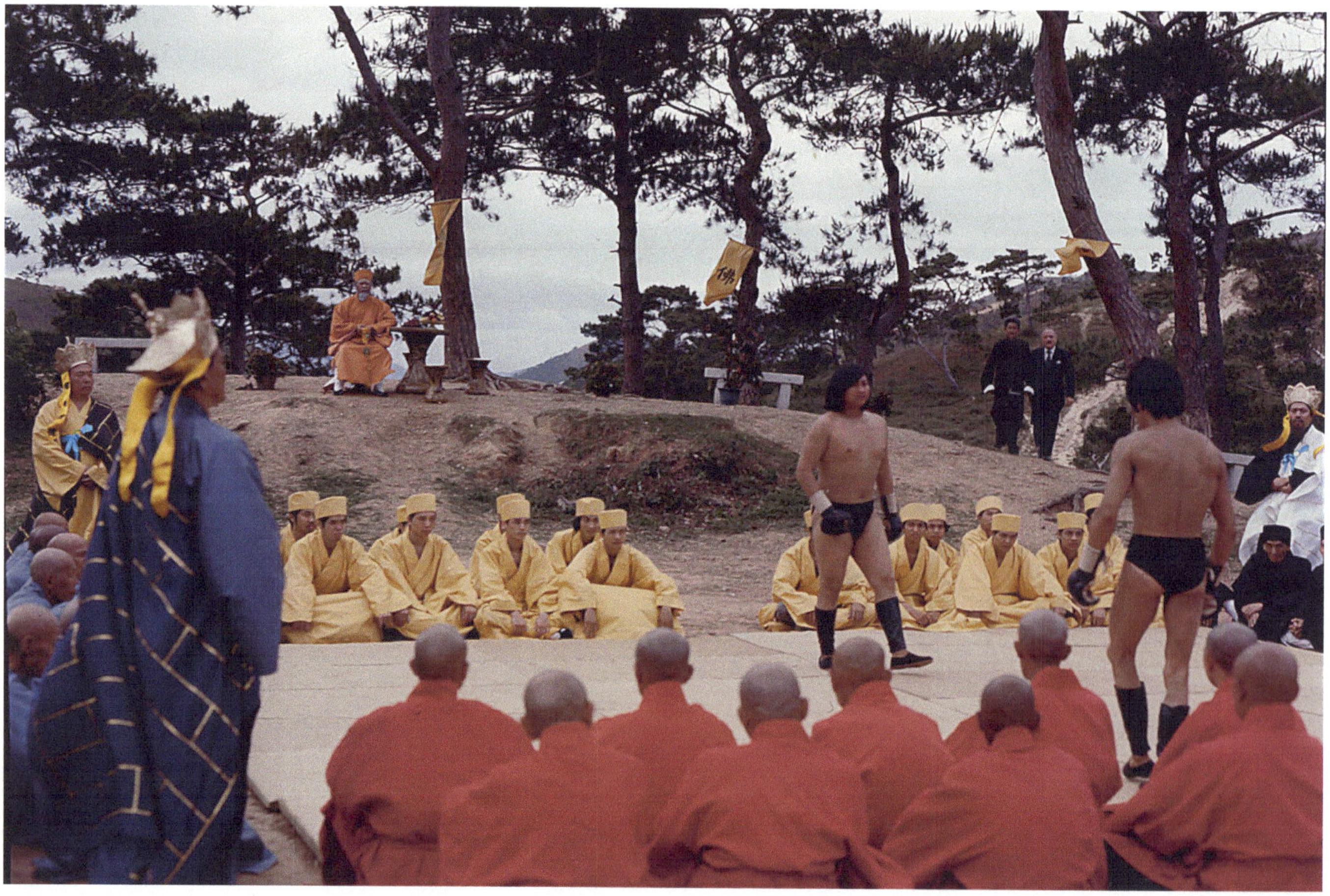

Enter the Dragon Photographic Collection – Vol. 1

Enter the Dragon Photographic Collection – Vol. 1

14  *Enter the Dragon* Photographic Collection – Vol. 1

Enter the Dragon Photographic Collection – Vol. 1

Enter the Dragon Photographic Collection – Vol. 1

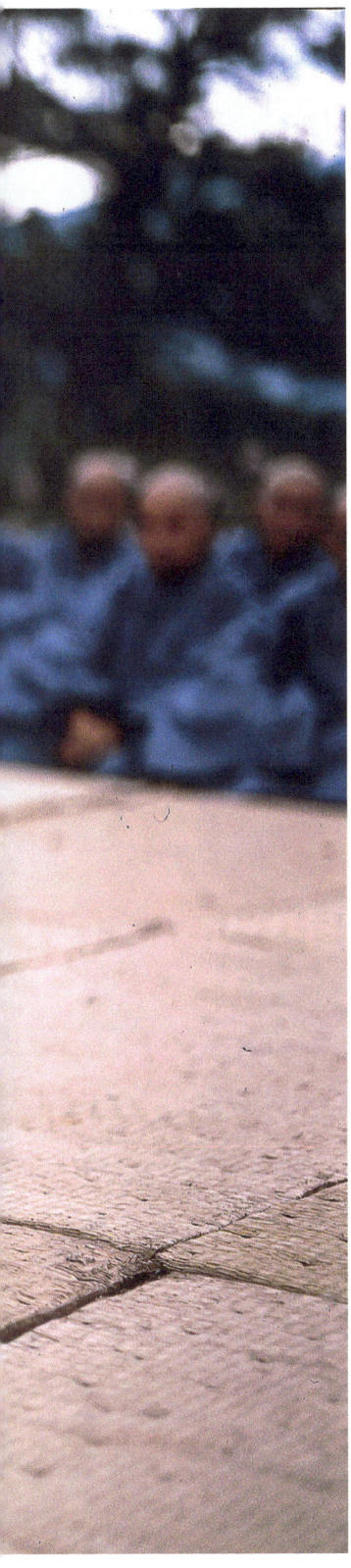

# A MEETING WITH THE ABBOT

Enter the Dragon Photographic Collection – Vol. 1

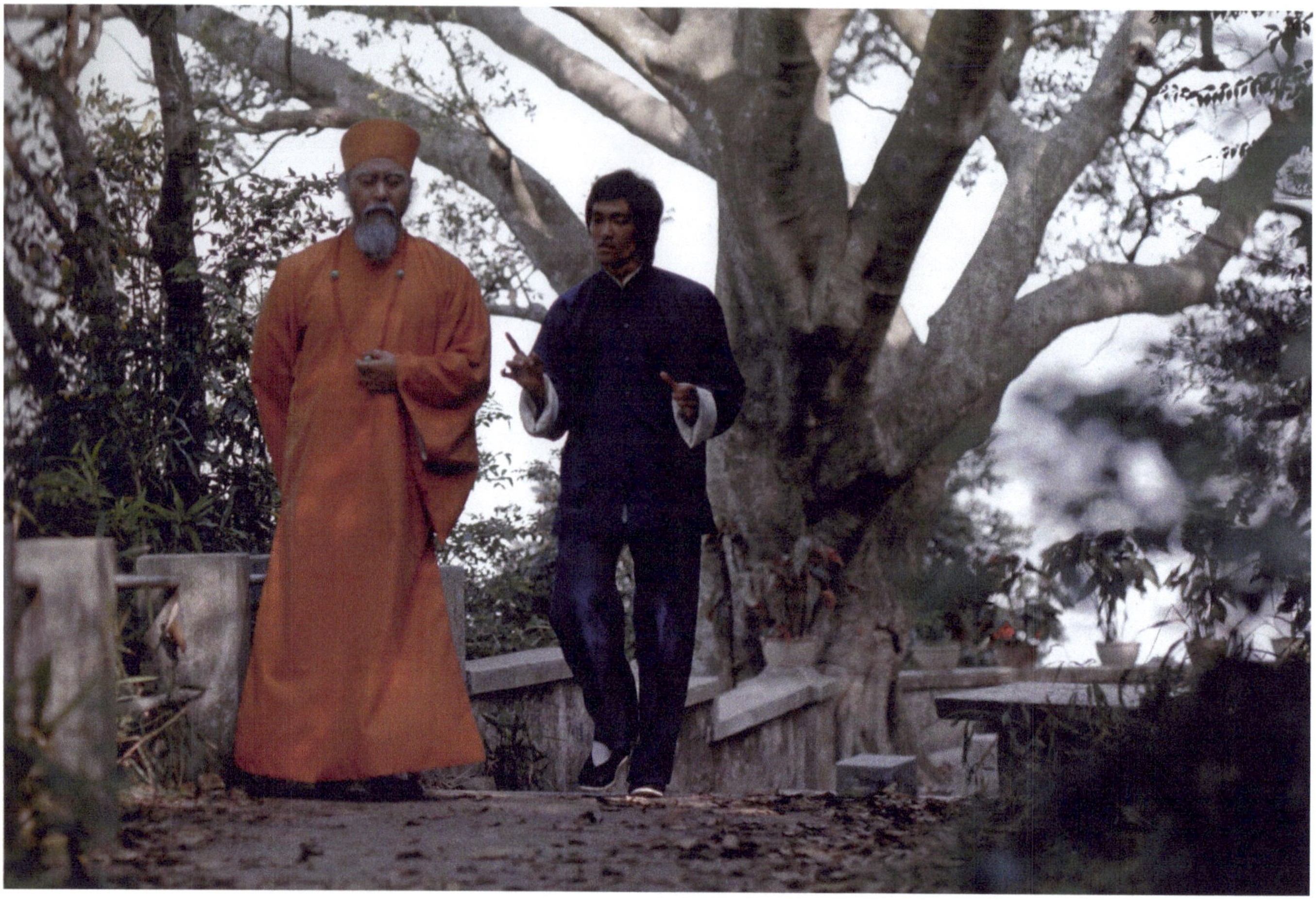

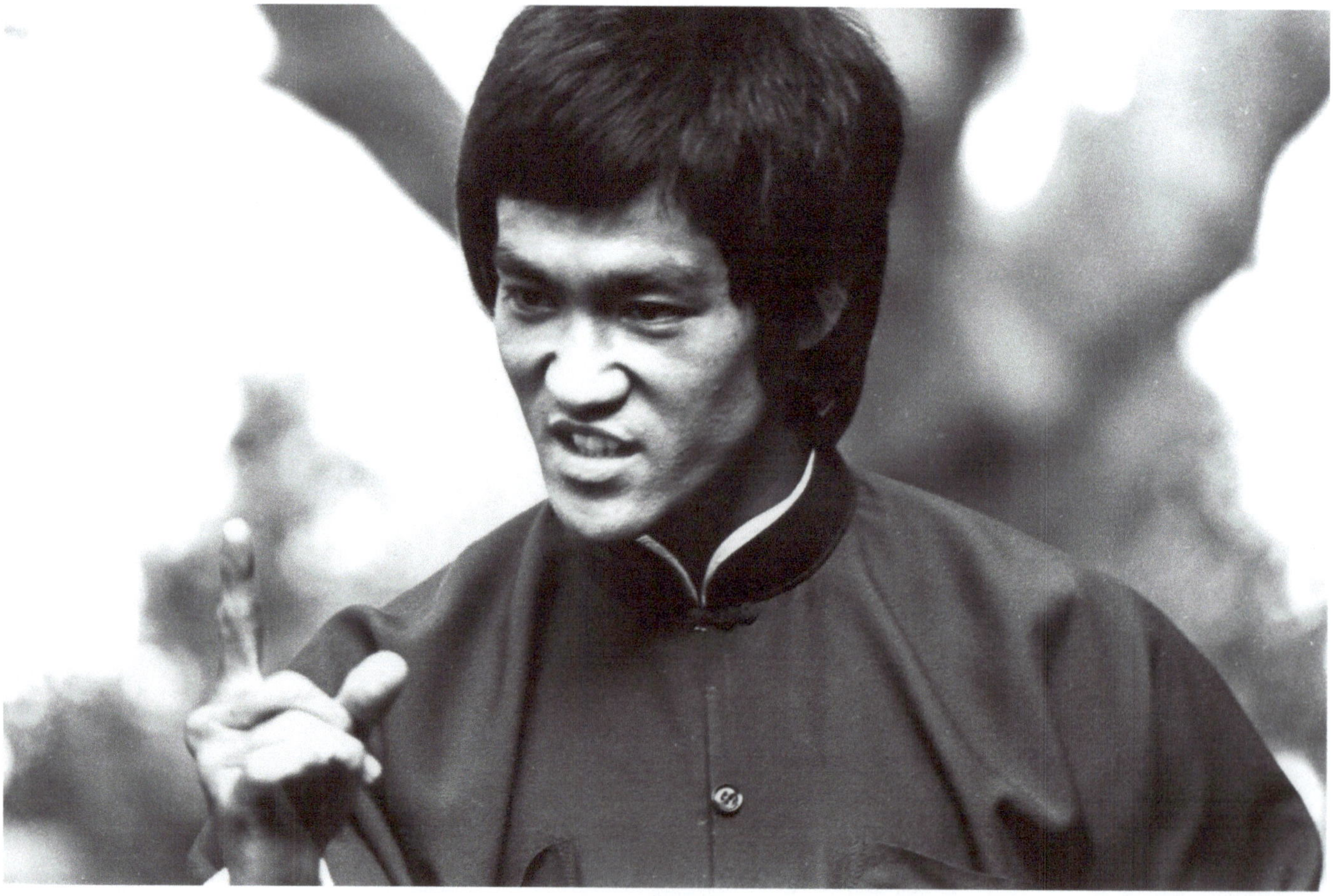

# THE MISSION

*Enter the Dragon* Photographic Collection – Vol. 1

# THE BOAT

*Enter the Dragon* Photographic Collection – Vol. 1

Enter the Dragon Photographic Collection – Vol. 1

Enter the Dragon Photographic Collection – Vol. 1

# "DON'T CONCENTRATE ON THE FINGER"

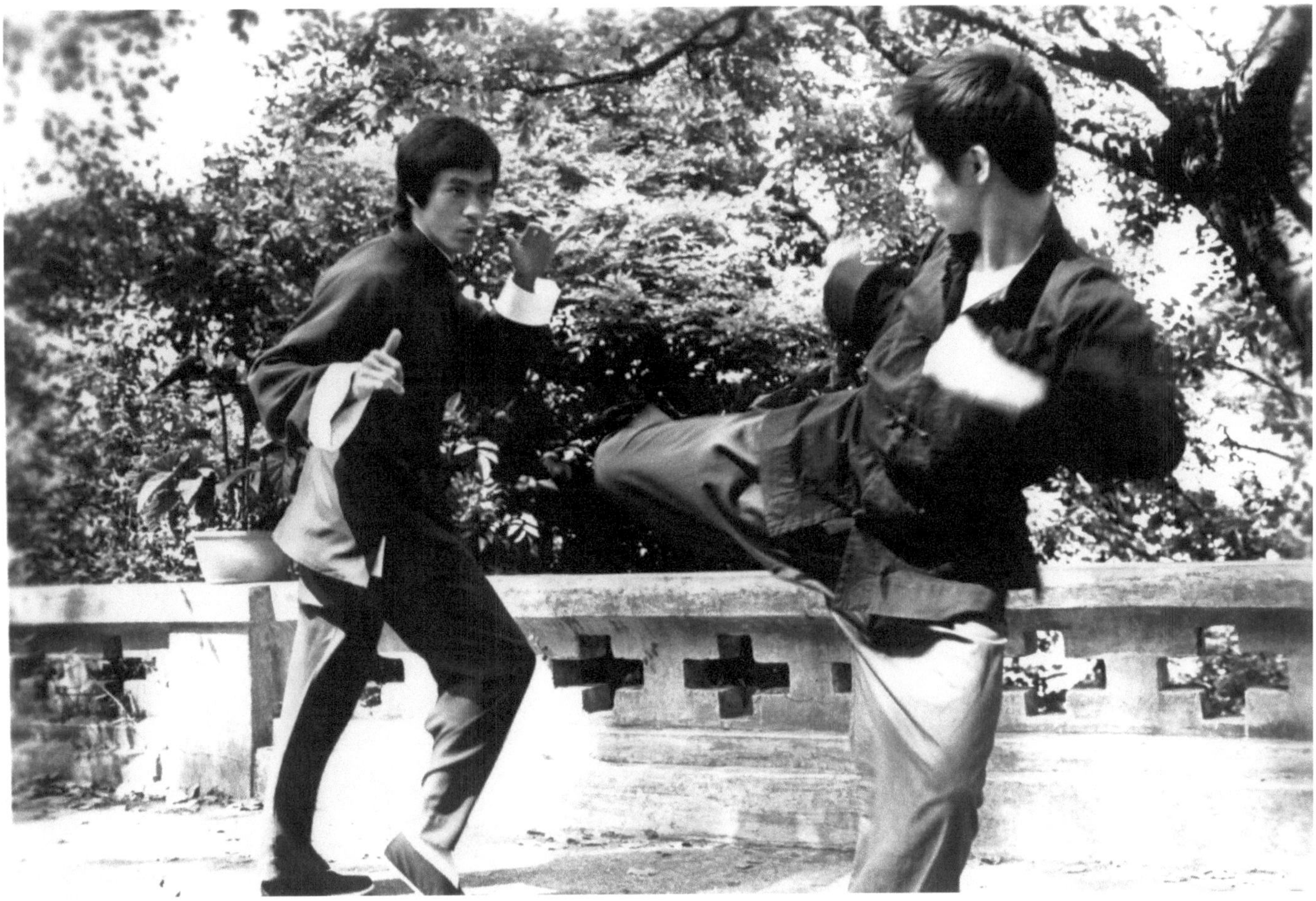

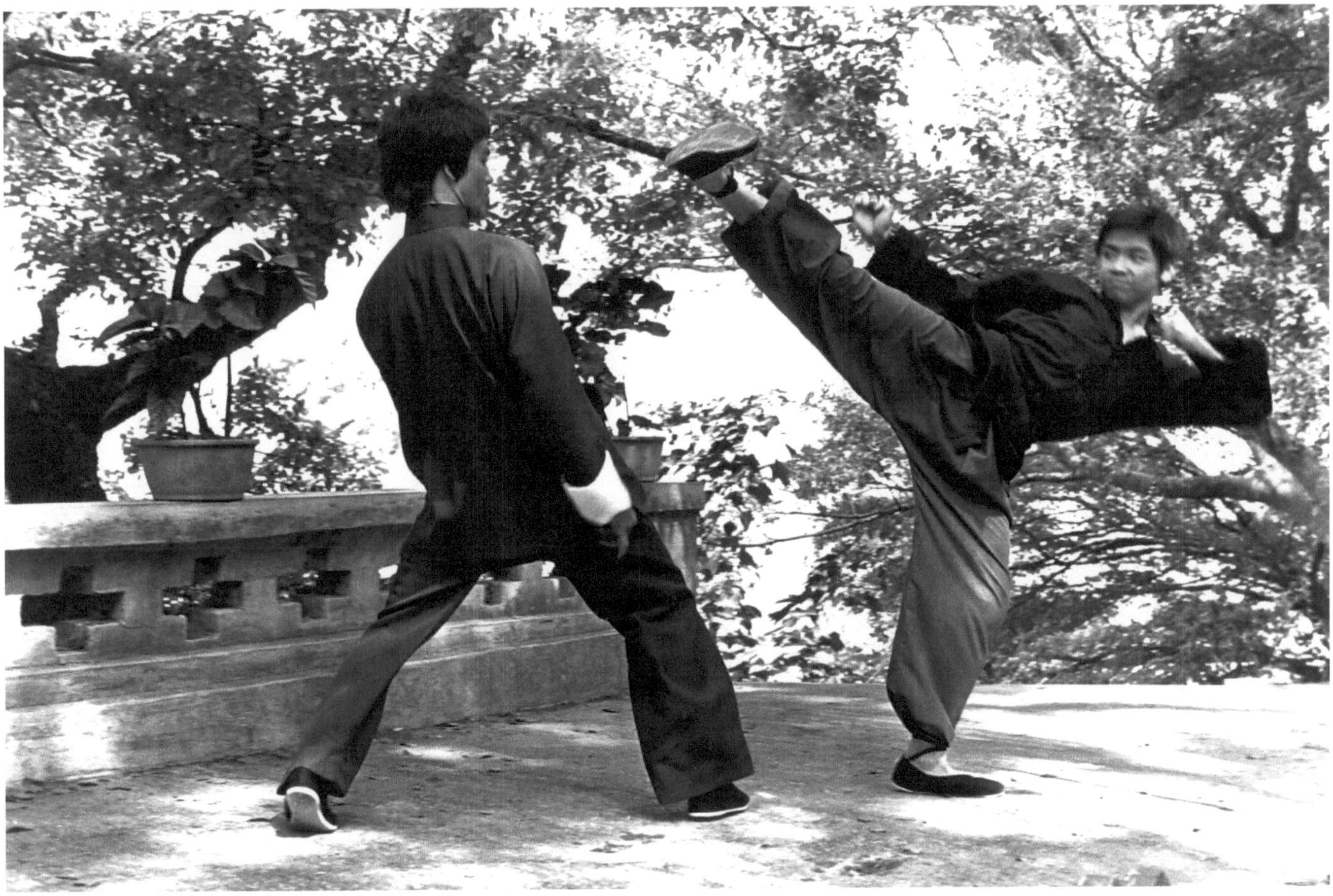

Another iconic moment is when Lee gives his young student Lao a lesson. The actor playing him is Stephen Tung Wei who also went on to become an accomplished actor stuntman and fight chorographer, who we know for his work on many films including *Hard Boiled* (1992), *The Accidental Spy* (2001) and *Operation Mekong* (2016).

# "WHAT'SH YOUR SHTYLE?"

# WELCOME TO HAN'S ISLAND

40  *Enter the Dragon* Photographic Collection – Vol. 1

Roper, Williams and Lee seem distracted as they Tanya welcomes them to Han's Island. Was there attention drawn to Bolo disposing of a body being thrown into the sea?

# PREPARING THE BANQUET

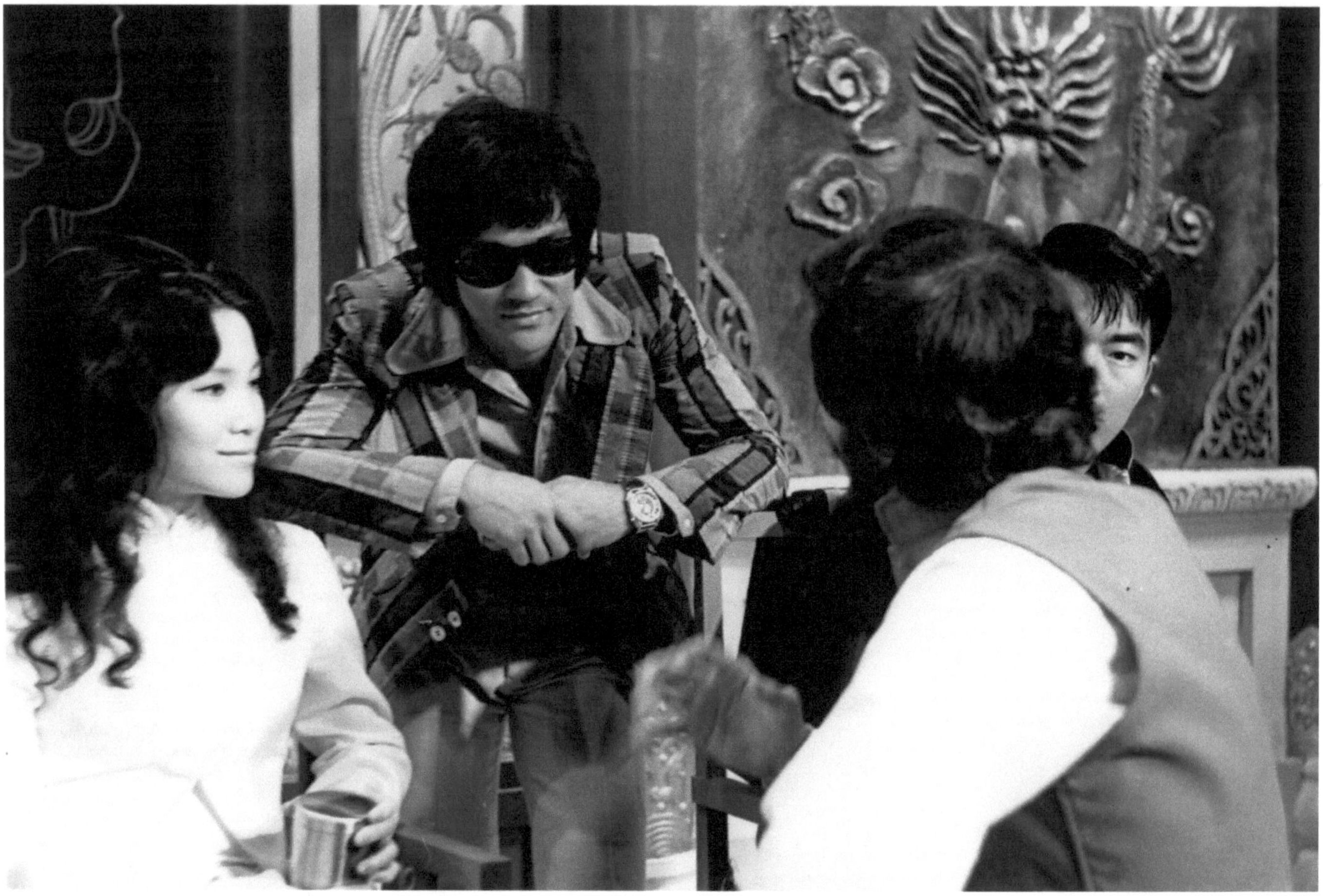

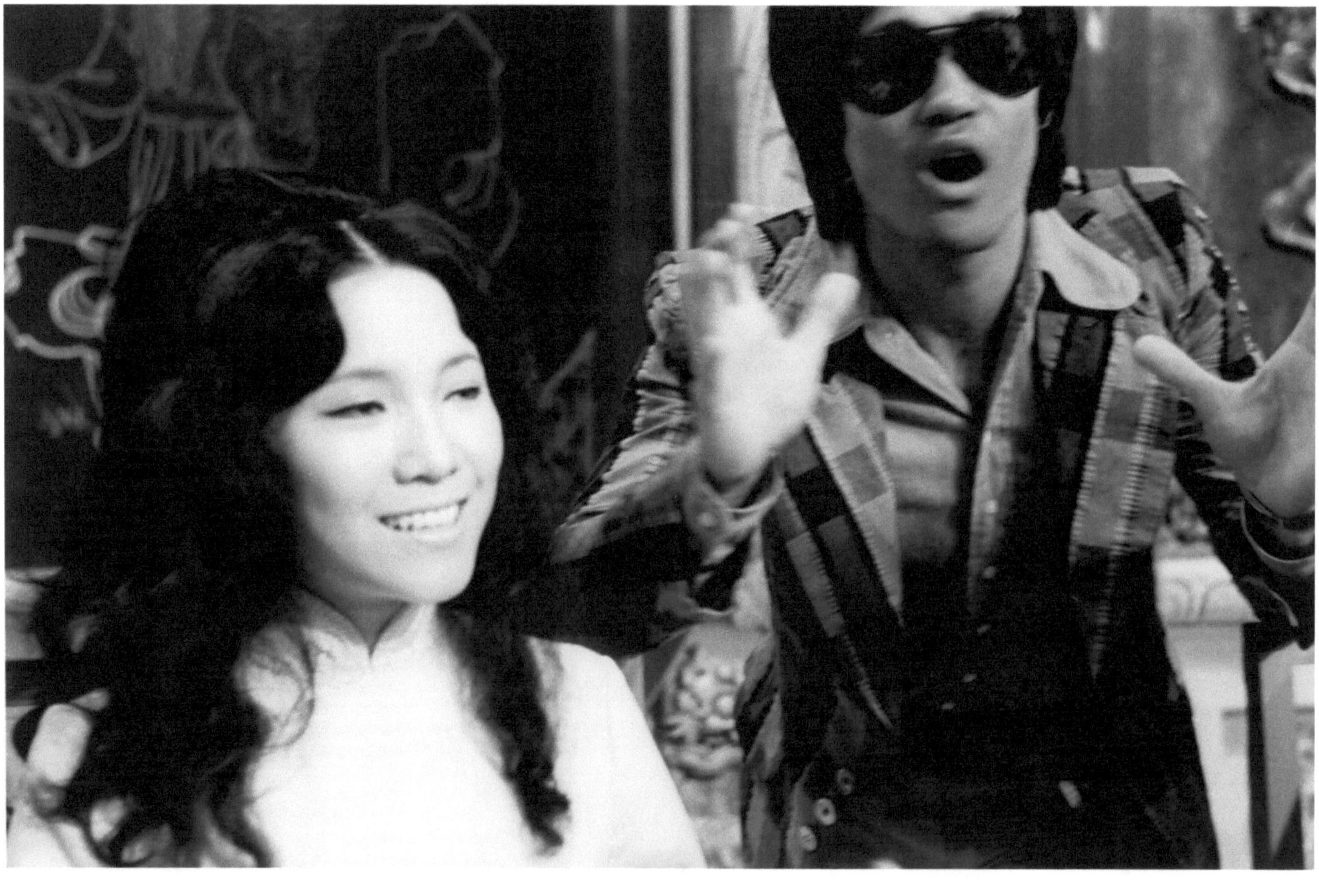

# MORNING EDIFICATION

*Enter the Dragon* Photographic Collection – Vol. 1

48  *Enter the Dragon* Photographic Collection – Vol. 1

# JIM KELLY GETS A LESSON

Enter the Dragon Photographic Collection – Vol. 1      51

# YUEN WAH AS BRUCE LEE

When we first saw *Enter the Dragon* we were impressed with Bruce's acrobatic abilities.

But we were to learn that he was doubled by Yuen Wah who skilfully mimicked Bruce fooling cinema audiences when first screened.

Enter the Dragon Photographic Collection – Vol. 1        53

# BOARDS DON'T HIT BACK!

*Enter the Dragon* Photographic Collection – Vol. 1

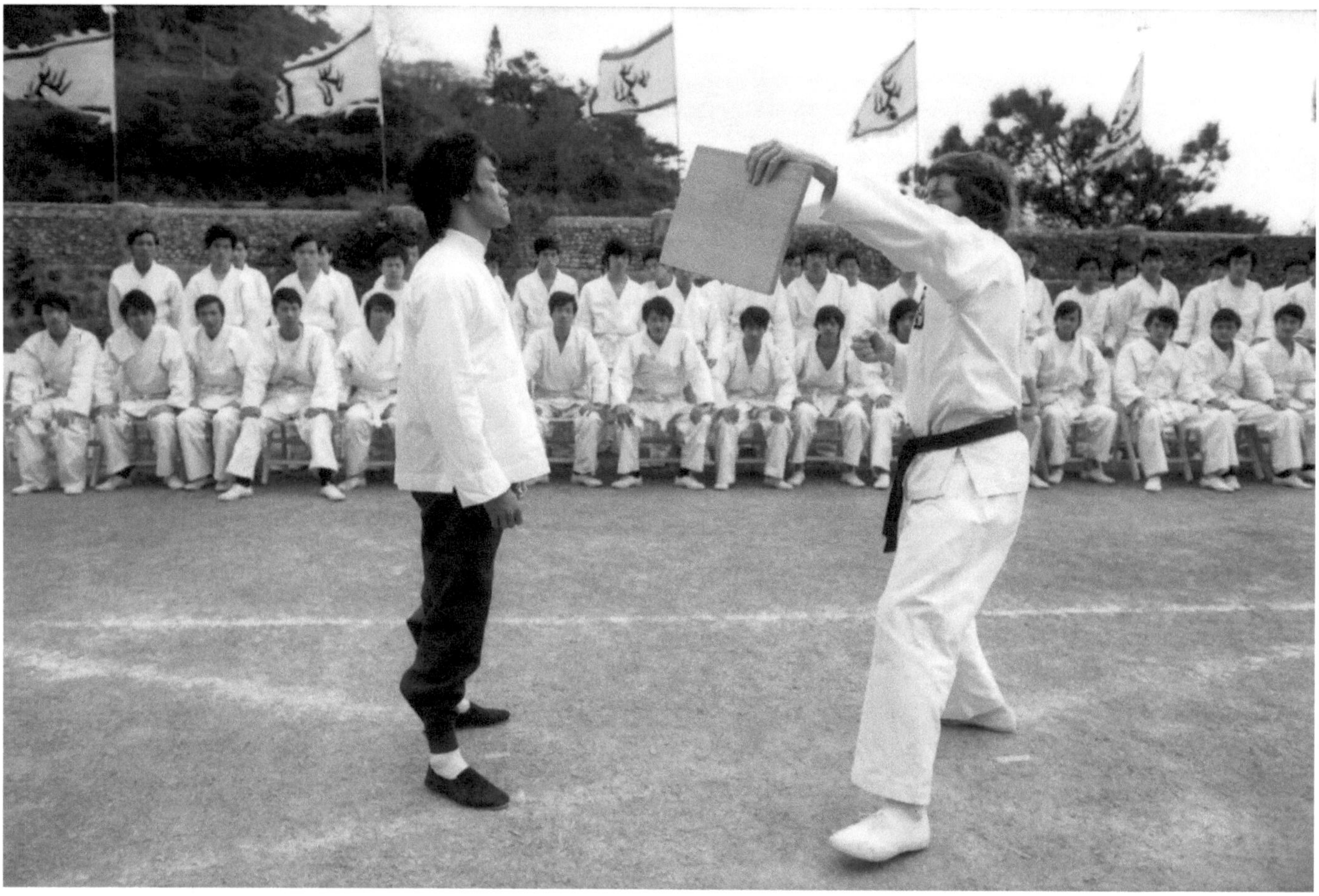

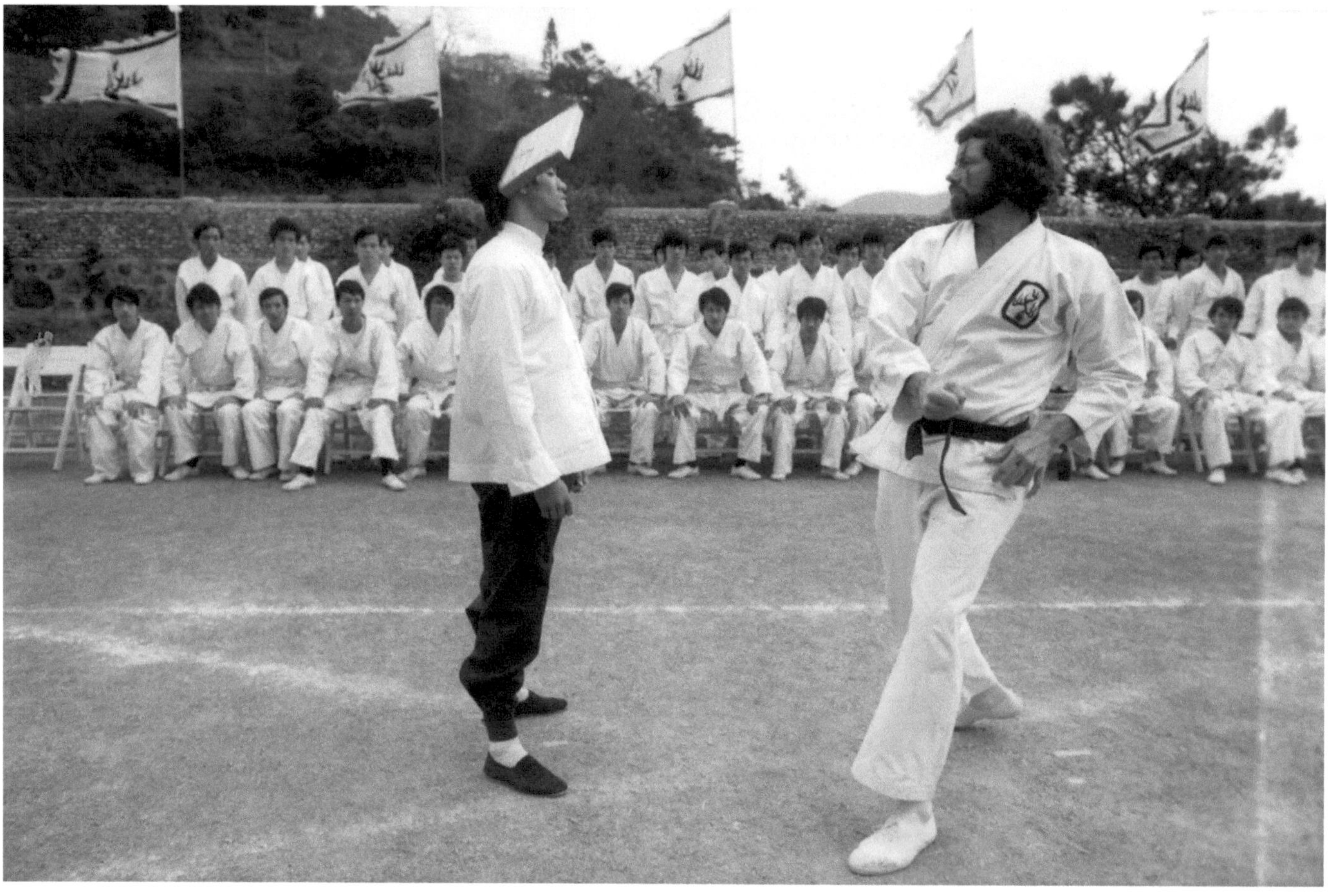

Enter the Dragon Photographic Collection – Vol. 1

# THE ART OF FIGHTING, WITH FIGHTING!

Enter the Dragon Photographic Collection – Vol. 1

# CASING OUT HAN'S ISLAND

Lee cases out the island, stealthily dressed in black, only to be spotted by Williams who comments...

" A Human Fly".

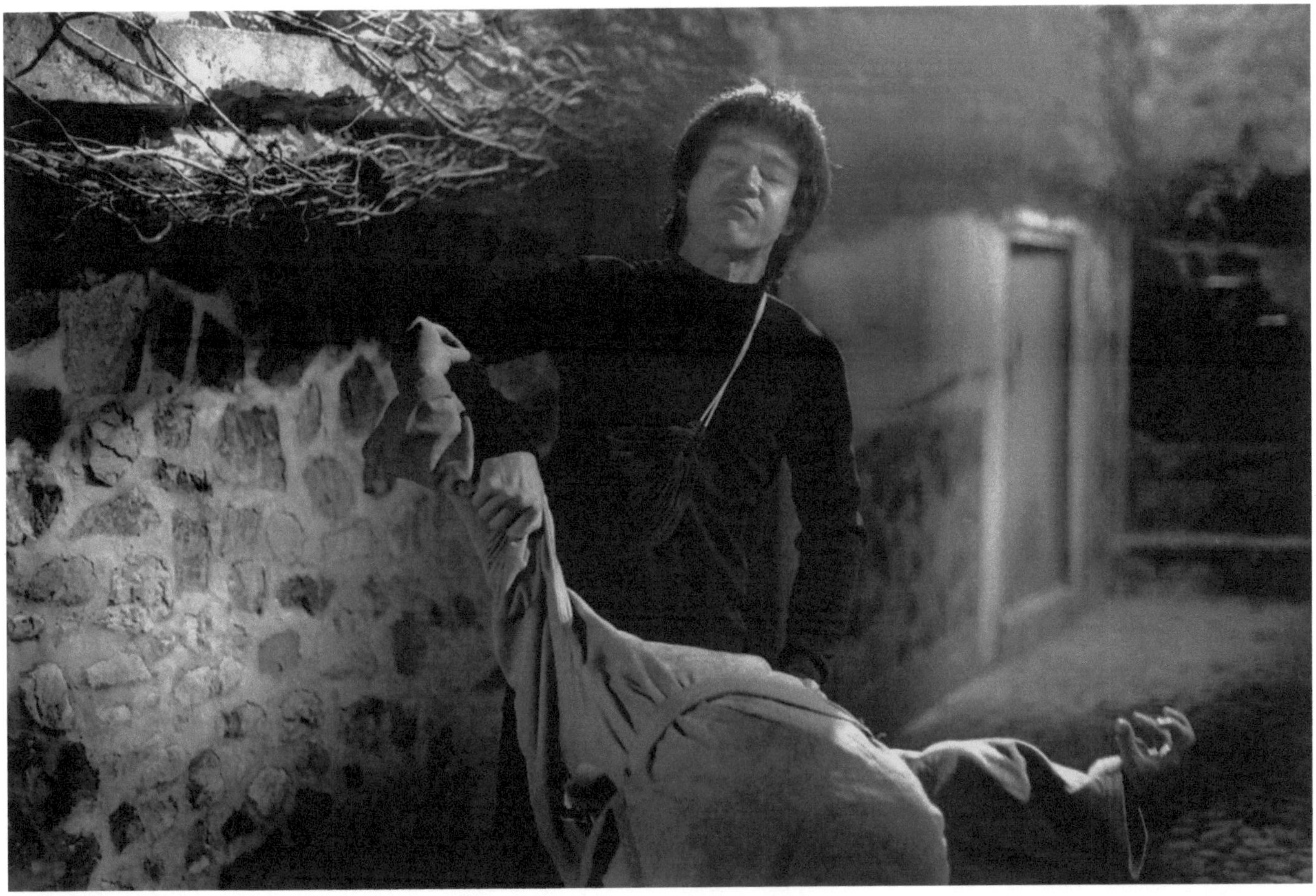

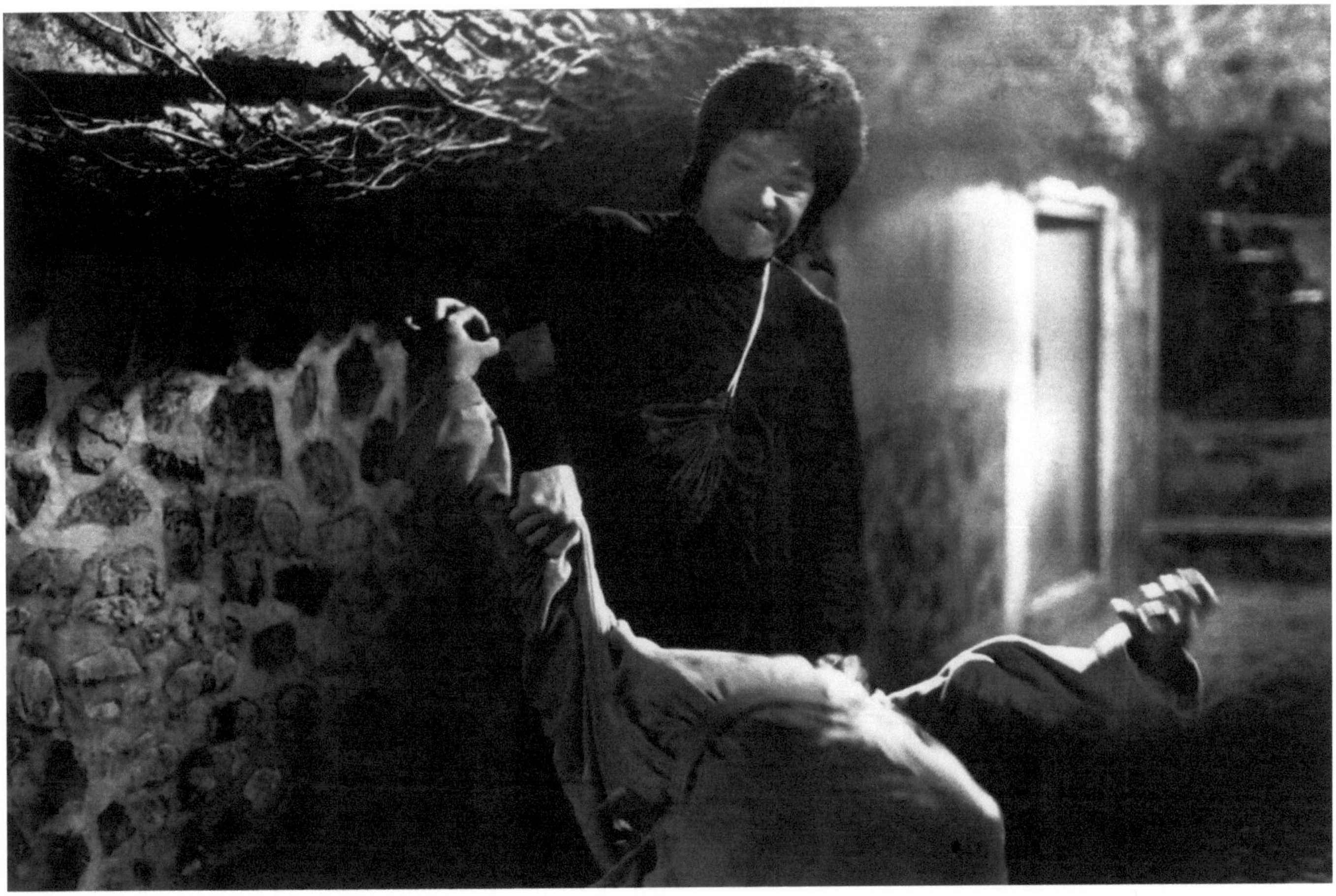

*Enter the Dragon* Photographic Collection – Vol. 1

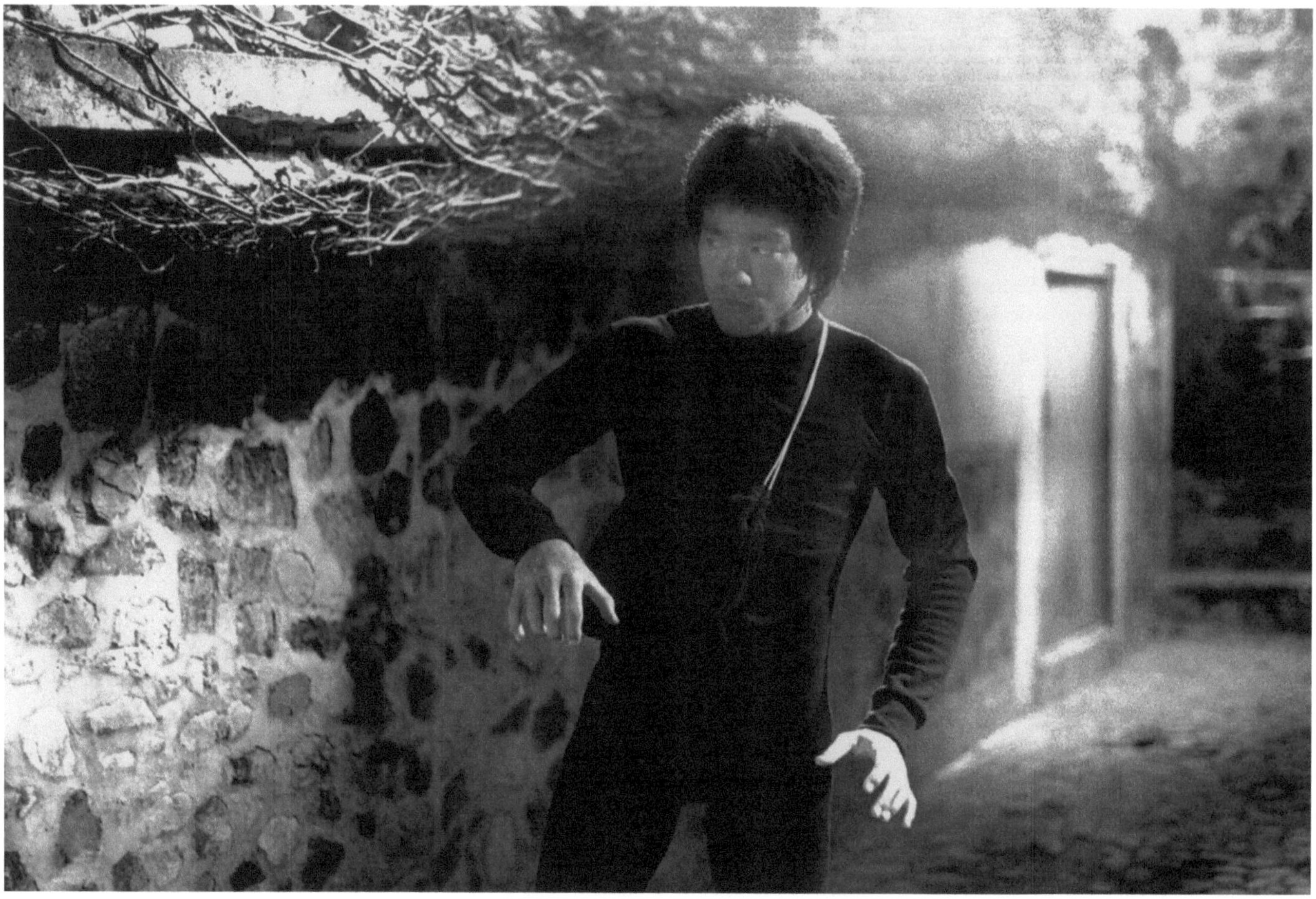

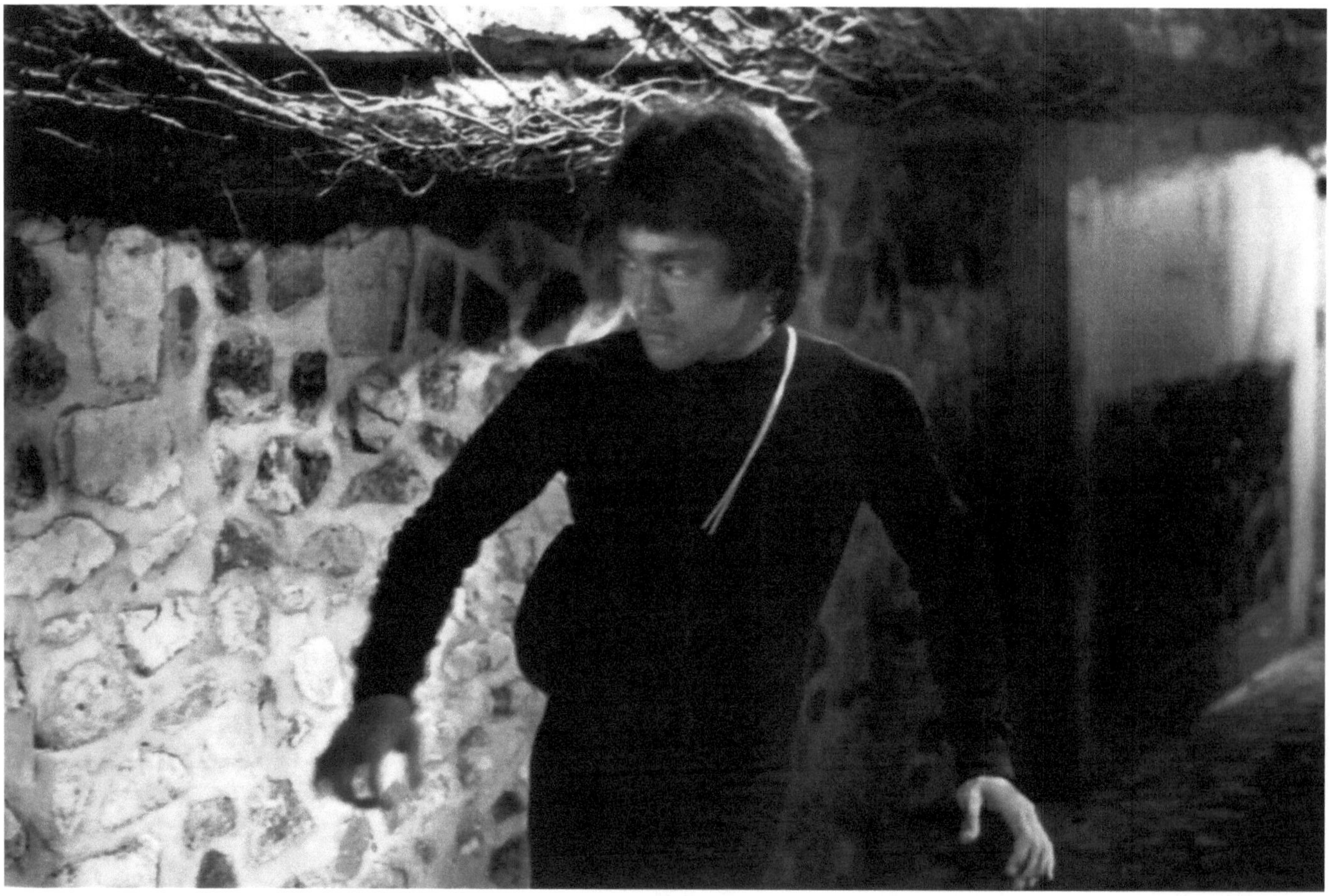

Enter the Dragon Photographic Collection – Vol. 1

64  *Enter the Dragon* Photographic Collection – Vol. 1

*Enter the Dragon* Photographic Collection – Vol. 1

# BRUCE VERSUS BOLO

Enter the Dragon Photographic Collection – Vol. 1

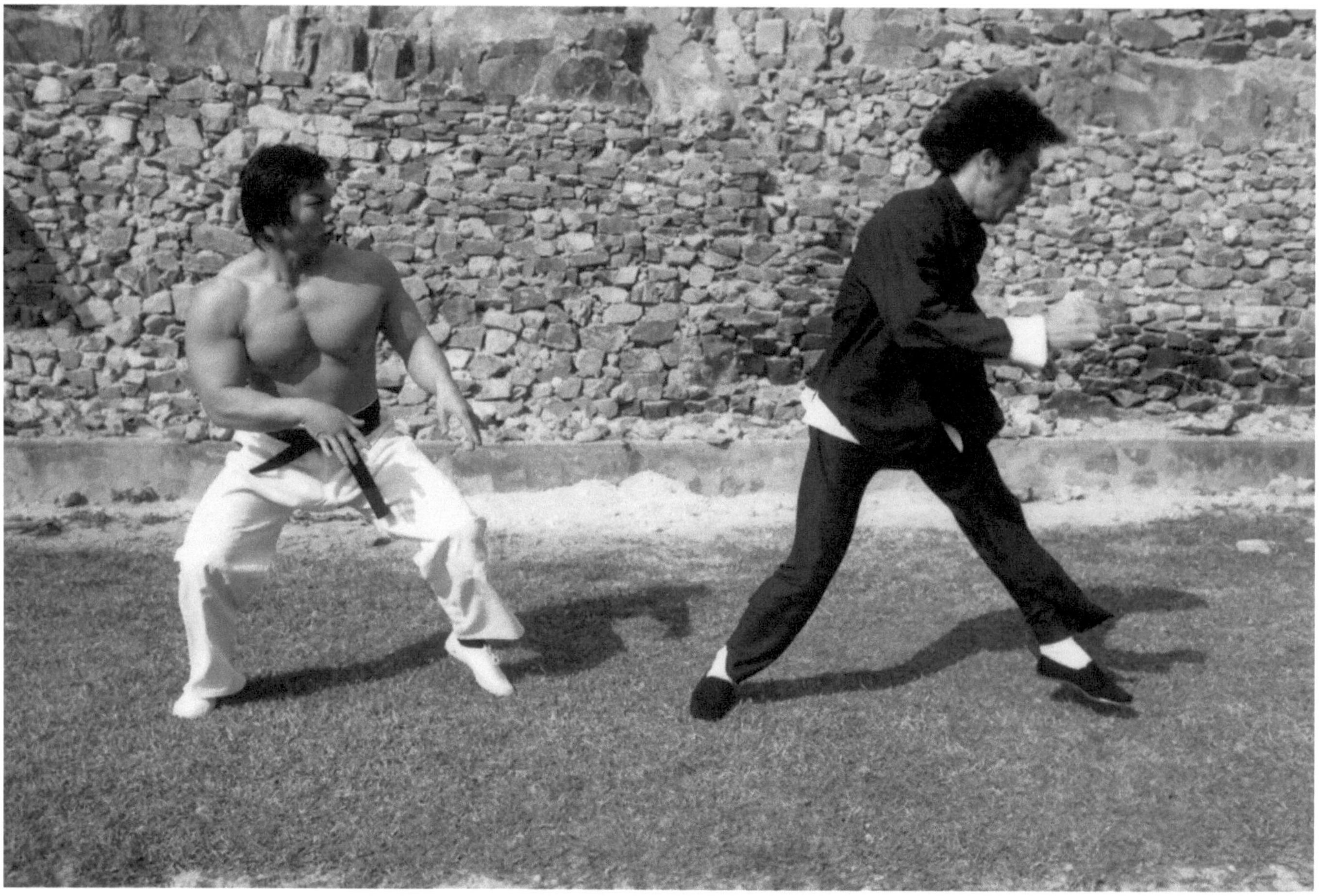

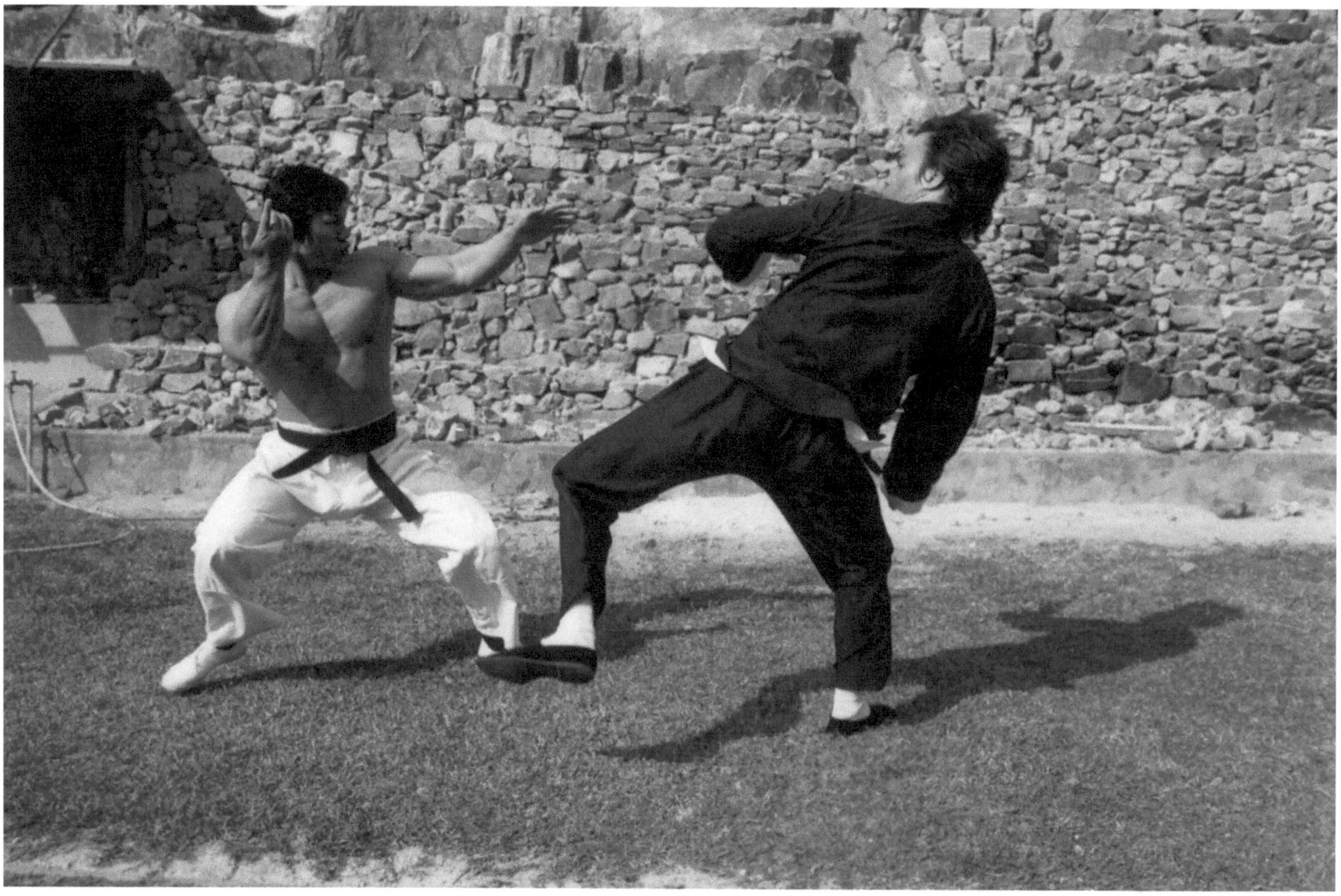

Enter the Dragon Photographic Collection – Vol. 1

# THE POWER OF THE KICK

Enter the Dragon Photographic Collection – Vol. 1

That kick looked real, and according to Bob Wall Bruce "it was". "Bruce liked sparring with me because I could take the impact when he threw kicks at me which allowed us to make this shot look totally real, and despite rumours I had no padding on for the shot".

# YUEN WAH GETS A LESSON

Enter the Dragon Photographic Collection – Vol. 1

# CUT BY THE BROKEN BOTTLE

**B**ob Wall said "To shoot the scene, I had to break real bottles. And Bruce had instructed me to take the jacket edge of my right hand which I one in each hand. But lunge with the right hand at his left peck. Bruce's words were come at me as fast as you can. So when we went for the sixth take, Bruce had his right hand up and he just began to spin. And as he spins, he jammed his right fist into the glass. And so Fred Weintraub called me and said you know there's a rumour that Bruce is going to kill you".

# SPARRING WITH BOB WALL OFF-SET

Bob enjoyed sparring with Bruce. He once said "Let's get something straight, Bruce was the real deal, I know a lot of people who only thinks he was good on screen. But they were wrong, dead wrong! If you sparred with Bruce you found out the hard way and just how wrong they were!"

Enter the Dragon Photographic Collection – Vol. 1

# WATCHING REHEARSALS

Bruce was constantly on set. Even when not filming he was always walking around and watching the cast as they were being filmed. Forever the perfectionist, observing and adding anything of value he could that would enhance the fight scenes.

Enter the Dragon Photographic Collection – Vol. 1

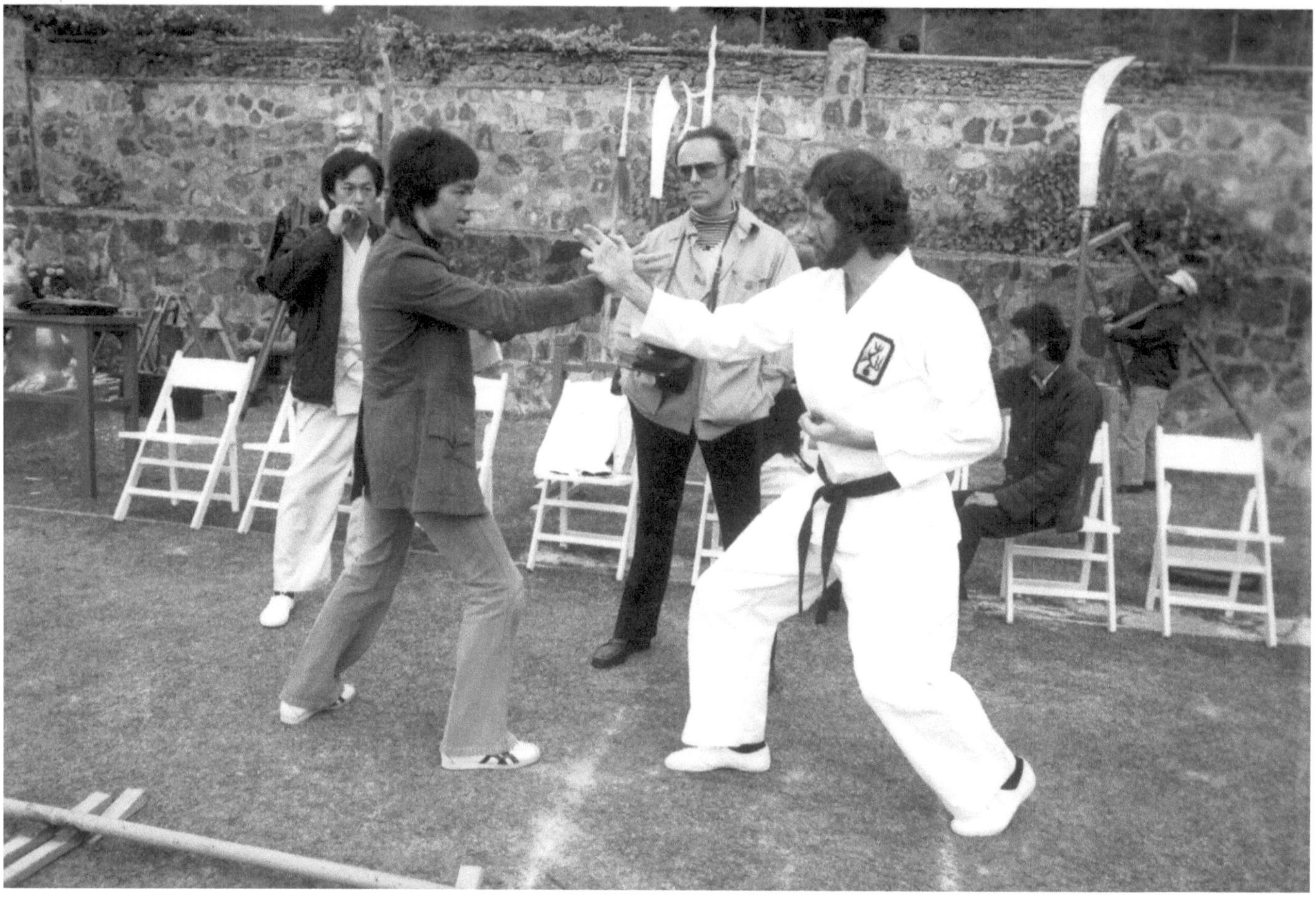

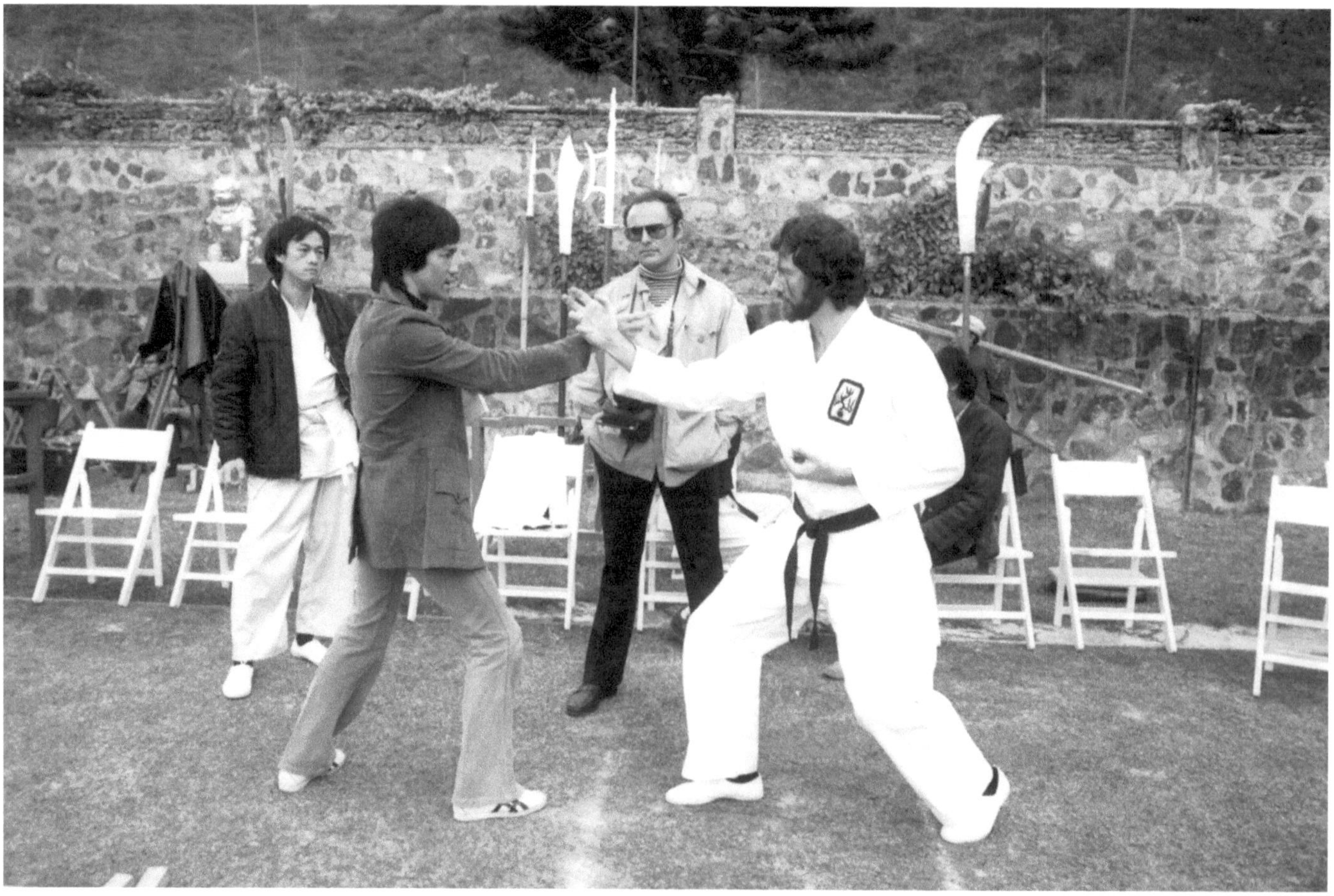

Enter the Dragon Photographic Collection – Vol. 1

# FINE-TUNING JIM KELLY

Bruce would often spar with cast members. Jim said of sparring with Bruce, "I have fought with the best, I have trained with the best, but in my opinion there has never been anyone like Bruce Lee, he was the best in the world".

Enter the Dragon Photographic Collection – Vol. 1

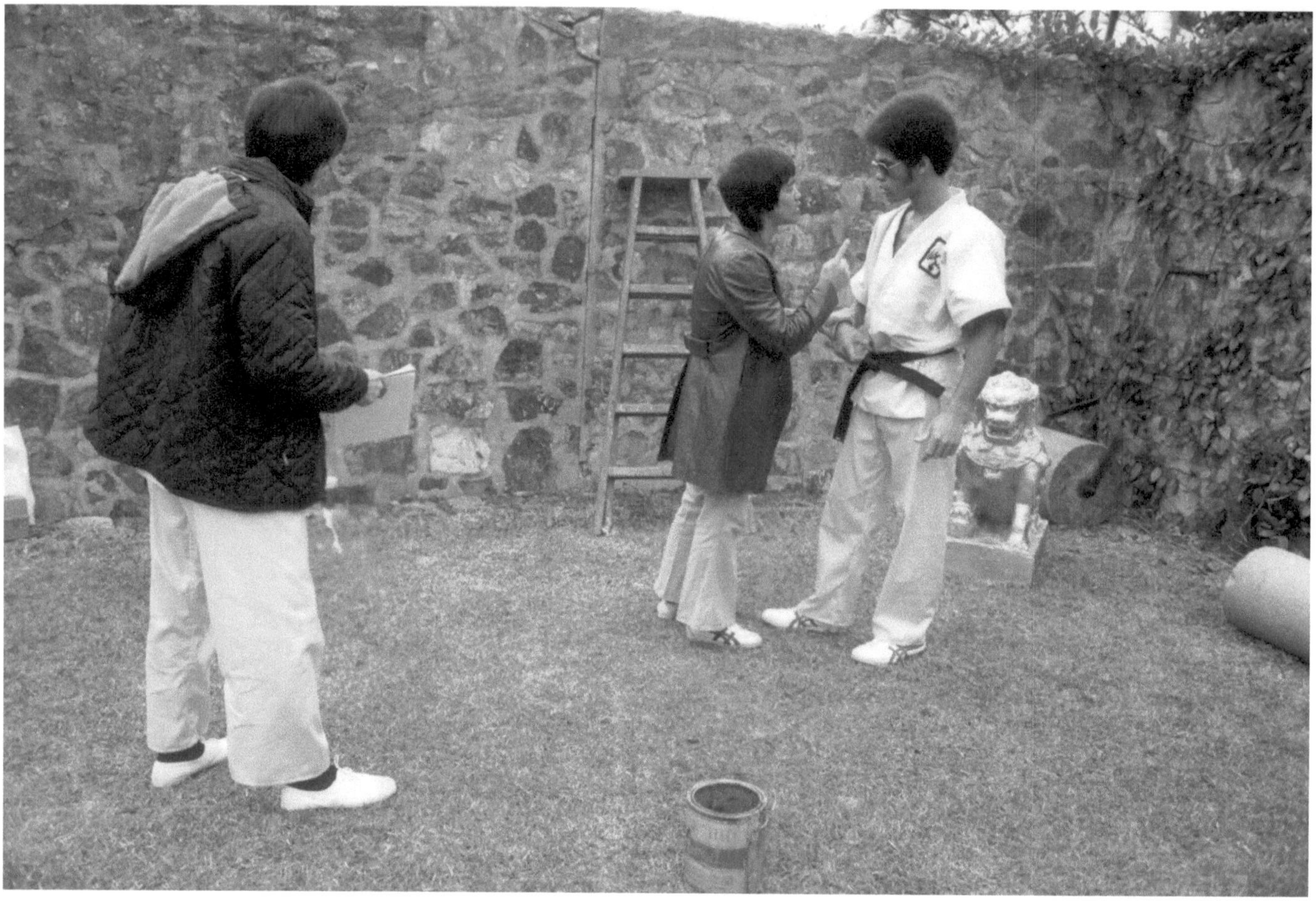

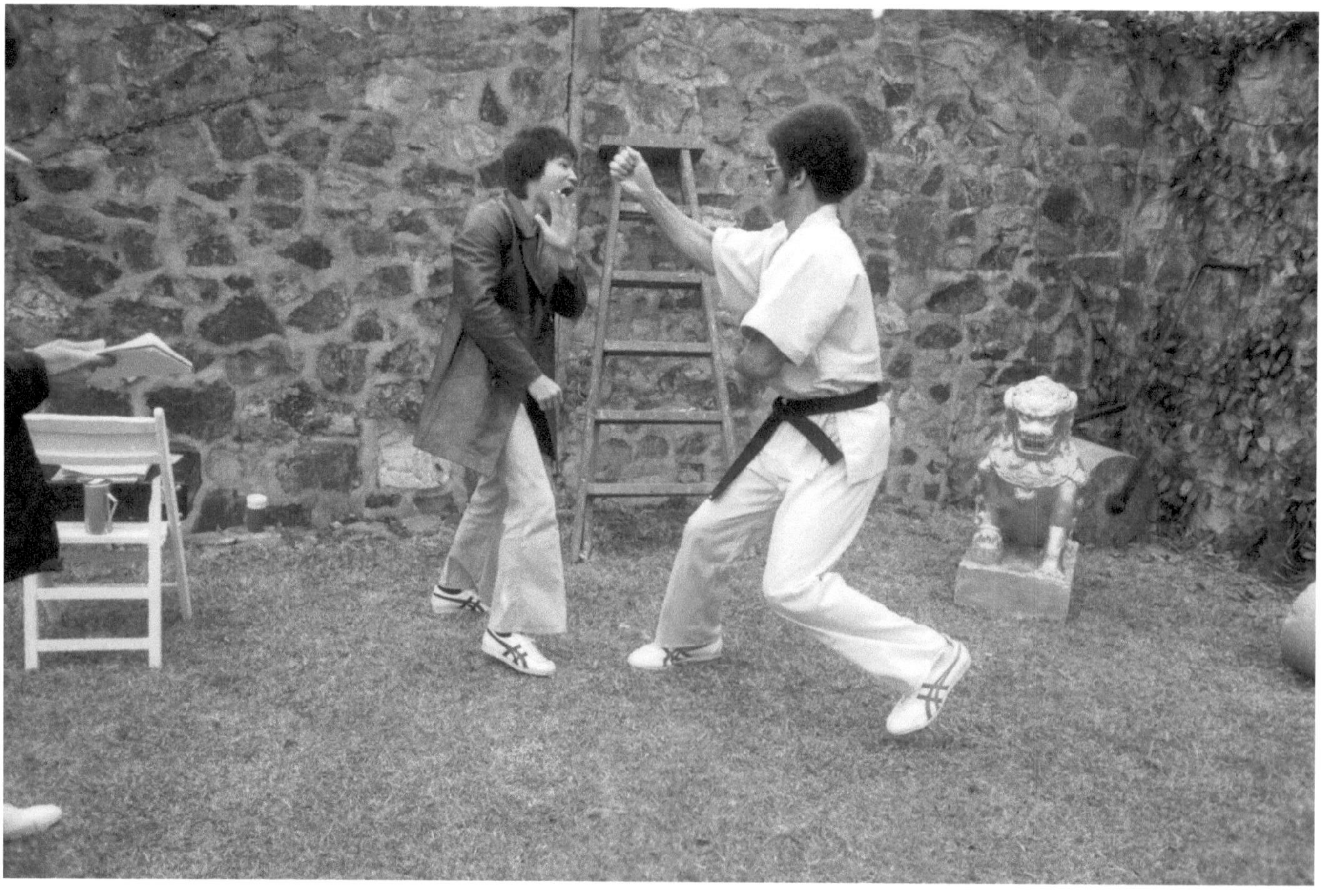

Enter the Dragon Photographic Collection – Vol. 1

# JACKIE CHAN VERSUS BRUCE LEE

Another iconic moment was the scene where Bruce dispatches Jackie Chan as one of the guards. Jackie at the time was a stuntman on the set. Jackie later said "he influenced me a lot, I admired him and the way he would talk, he could even speak English. Everyone on set thought he was God!"

# TWIRLING RODS OF IRON

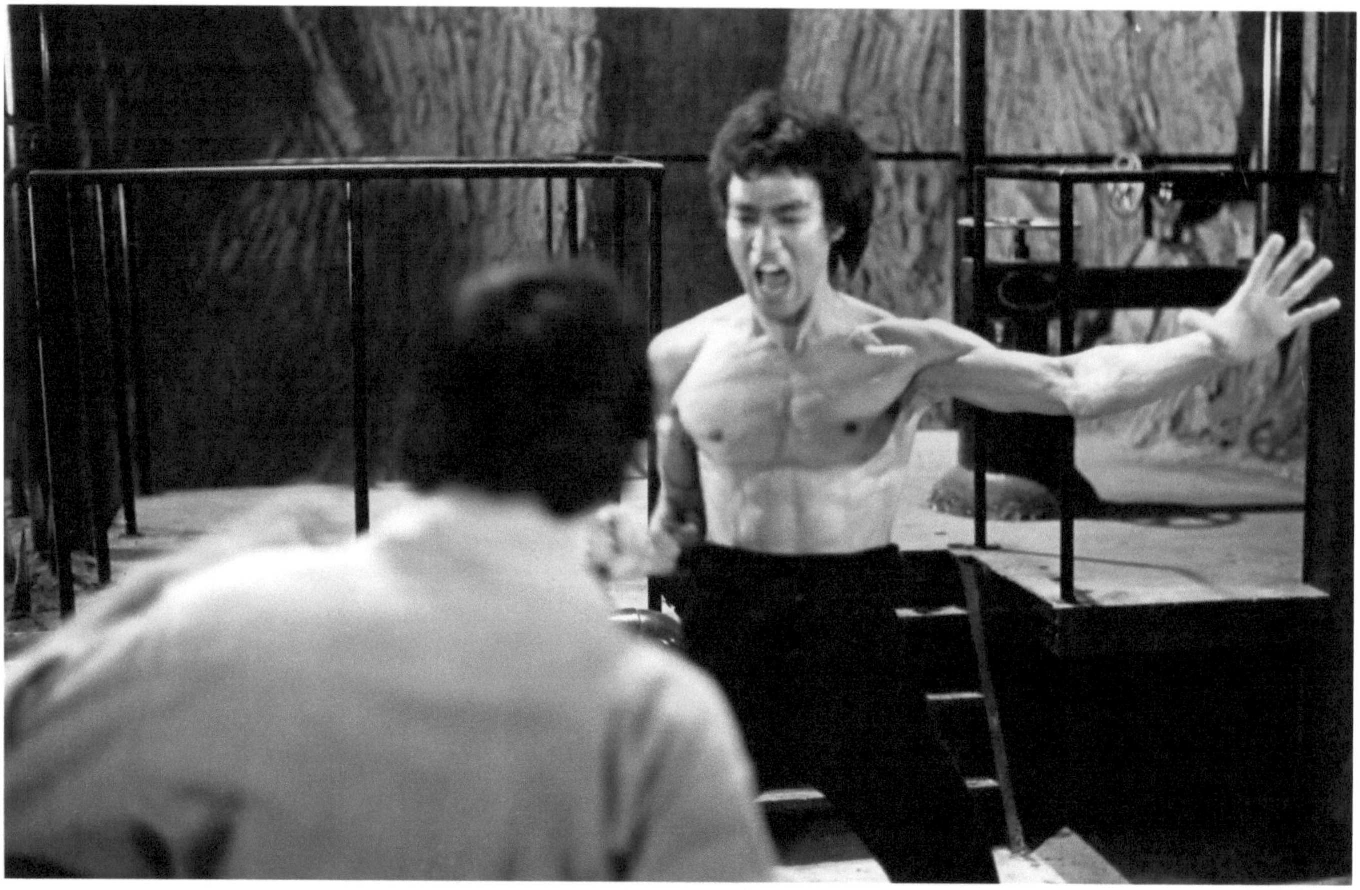

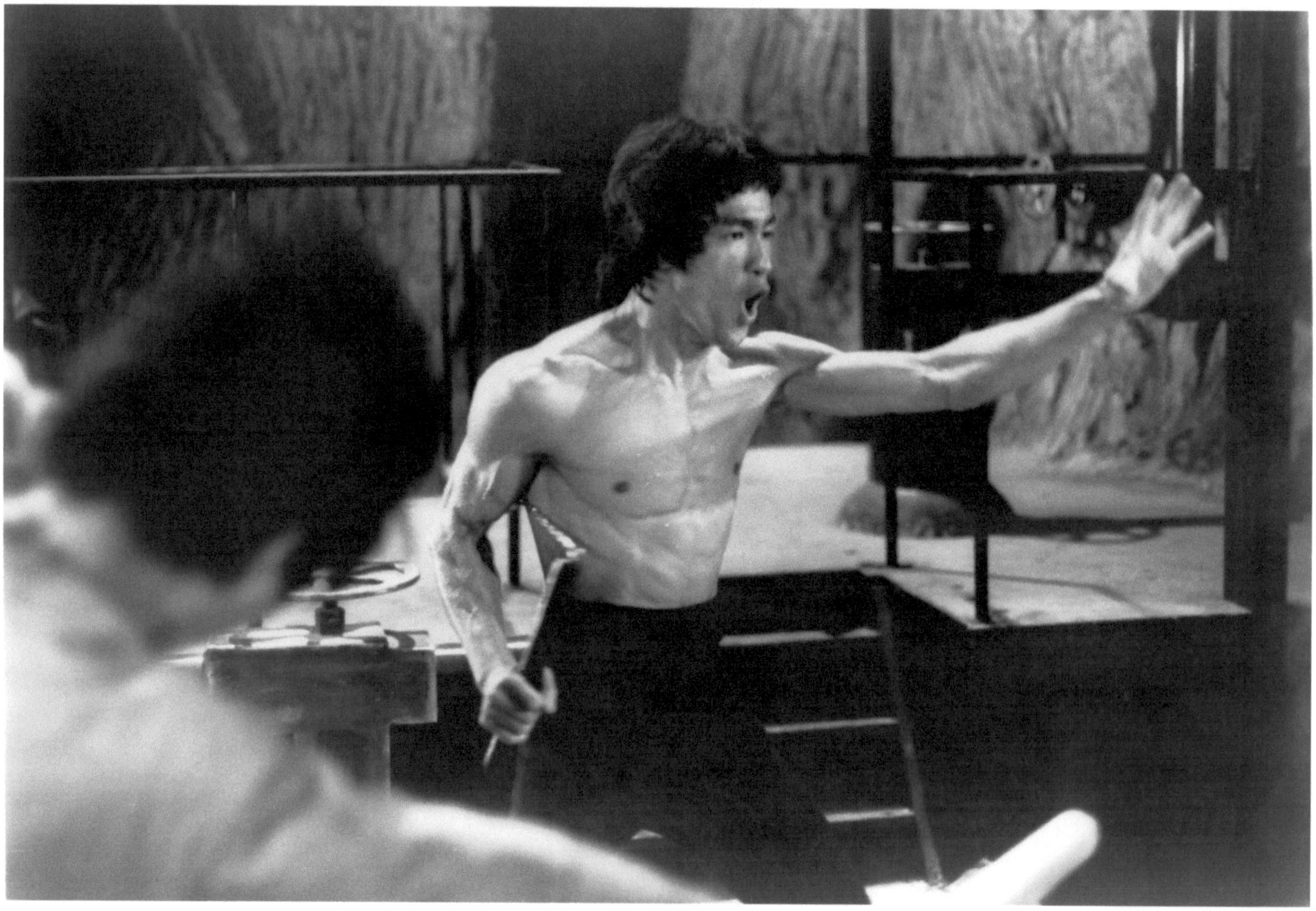

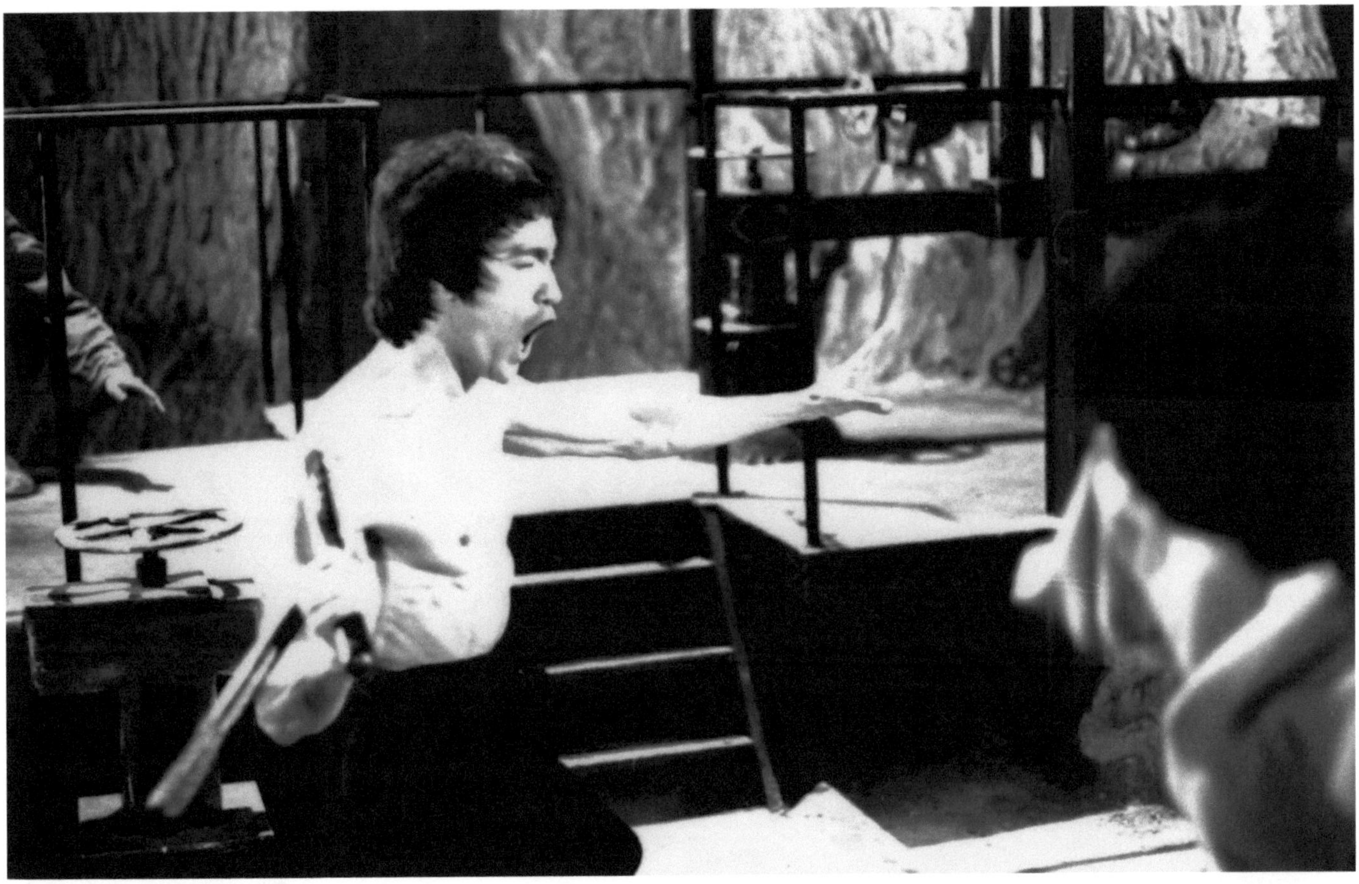

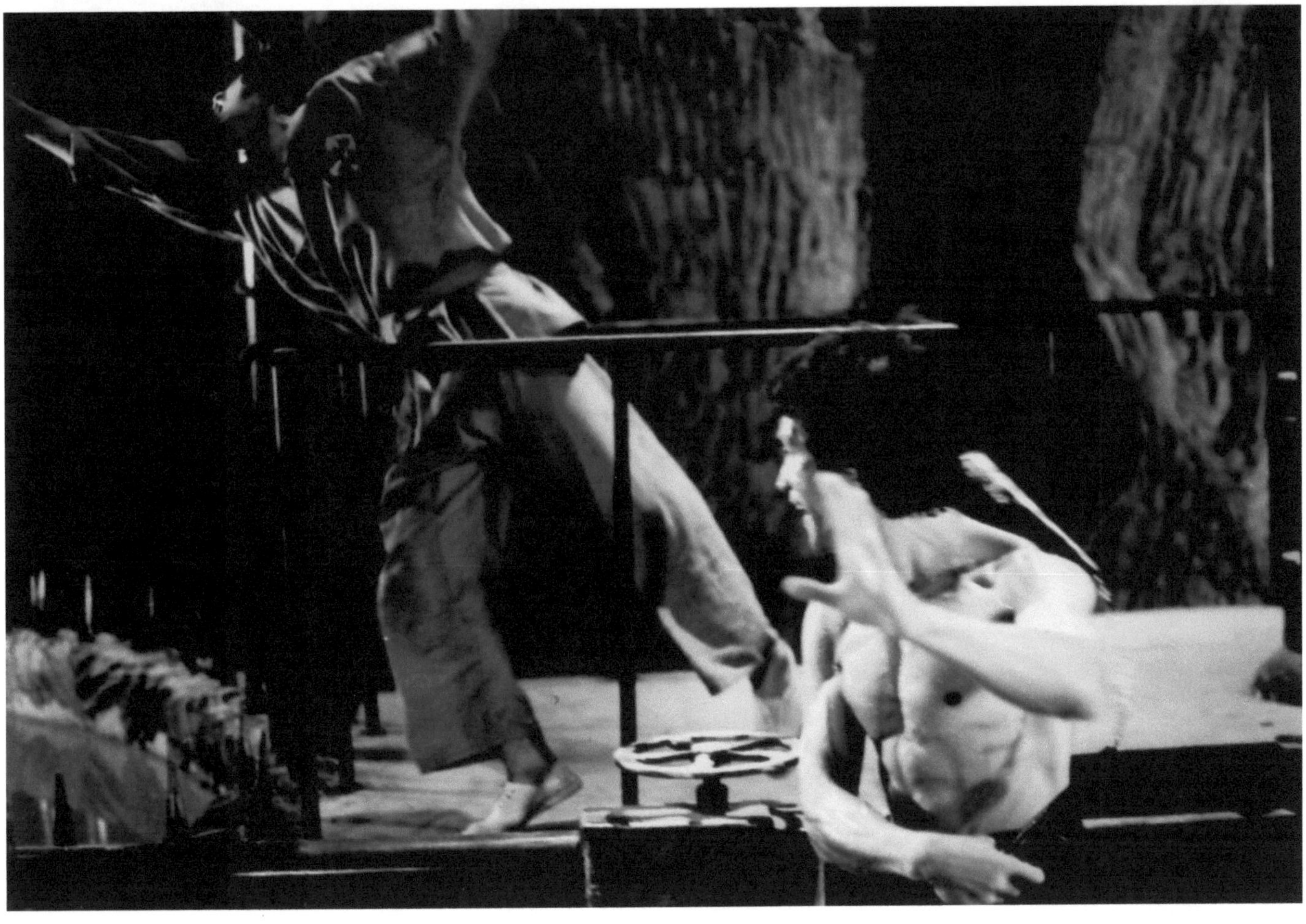

# THE DRAGON'S VICTORY SALUTE

www.ingramcontent.com/pod-product-compliance
Lightning Source LLC
Chambersburg PA
CBHW041506220426
43661CB00016B/1264